Facts

KU-750-421

Animal Rulers

KINGS OF THE SKIES

Rebecca Rissman

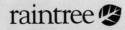

raintree

a Capstone company — publishers for children

Raintree is an imprint of Capstone Global Library Limited, a company incorporated in England and Wales having its registered office at 264 Banbury Road, Oxford, OX2 7DY – Registered company number: 6695582

www.raintree.co.uk
myorders@raintree.co.uk

Edited by Adrian Vigliano
Designed by Kayla Rossow
Picture research by Kelly Garvin
Production by Kathy McColley
Originated by Captsone Global Library Limited
Printed and bound in India

ISBN 978 1 4747 4862 9 (hardback)
21 20 19 18 17
10 9 8 7 6 5 4 3 2 1

ISBN 978 1 4747 4868 1
22 21 20 19 18
10 9 8 7 6 5 4 3 2 1

British Library Cataloguing in Publication Data
A full catalogue record for this book is available from the British Library.

Acknowledgements
We would like to thank the following for permission to reproduce photographs: Minden Pictures/Hugh Maynard/NPL 21; Shutterstock: Abi Warner, cover (top left), Apichart Meesri, 5, Cristian Gusa, 11, FotoRequest, cover (top right), 19, iliuta goean, 13, lm stocker, cover (middle), Michal Ninger, 7, Ondrej Prosicky, 17, Tory Kallman, 15, Vladimir Hodac, cover (top middle), Vladimir Kogan Michael, 9, WorldWide, cover (bottom); artistic elements: Shutterstock: Alexandr Shevchenko, Anton Kudriashov, Creative Travel Projects, Evannovostro, Gallinago_media, Genova, Kauriana, KatarinaF, Kirill Smirnov, Lucie Rezna, Miceking, oorka, pixy_nook, Suphatthra China, Triff

We would like to thank Jackie Gai for her invaluable help in the preparation of this book.

Every effort has been made to contact copyright holders of material reproduced in this book. Any omissions will be rectified in subsequent printings if notice is given to the publisher.

Contents

Sky high animals

Heads up! The rulers of the skies are flying by.

These creatures have **adapted** to rule the skies. Some are fast. Some are loud. Others are skilled hunters. They are all amazing animals.

Rulers of the sky can be found all over the world. They live in many different types of **habitats**.

adapt change to fit into a new or different environment
habitat place where an animal can find its food, water, shelter and space to live

Northern goshawk

The forest is quiet. Suddenly a Northern goshawk dives. It grabs a rabbit. The hunt is over in seconds. Northern goshawks are huge **predators**. Their **wingspan** is nearly 1.2 metres (4 feet) wide. They have sharp **talons** and a strong beak. These birds live in North America, Europe and Asia.

predator animal that hunts other animals for food

wingspan distance between the tips of a pair of wings when fully open

talon raptor's sharp, curved claw; each toe has a talon

Fact! Northern goshawks have bright orange or red eyes.

Golden eagle

Golden eagles rule the skies in North America, Europe and Asia. These birds are fast and deadly. They can dive faster than 241 kilometres (150 miles) per hour. They have sharp talons. Golden eagles hunt for many types of animals. They eat small animals and large insects. Golden eagles sometimes even attack animals as large as deer.

Crow

Crows are found in North America, Asia
and Europe. Crows are usually all black.
These birds are known for being very clever.
Crows make tools and solve problems.
People have seen crows place walnuts
on roads. Cars crush the walnut shells.
Then crows swoop in to eat the nuts.

Great white pelican

Great white pelicans live in Europe, Asia and Africa. They rule ocean coastlines.

Great white pelicans are huge birds. Their wingspans can reach 3 metres (10 feet).

They can fly up to 483 kilometres (300 miles) without stopping.

These pelicans sometimes hunt in groups. They form a U-shape in the water and trap fish between them. Then they scoop up **prey**.

prey animal that is hunted by other animals for food

Albatross

Albatrosses live off the coast of every **continent** but Europe. Their wingspan can reach almost 3.6 metres (12 feet) across. Albatrosses fly up to 16,093 kilometres (10,000 miles) in one trip. And they hardly ever flap their wings! Albatrosses **glide** through the air. They can travel a long distance between each flap of their wings.

continent one of Earth's seven large land masses
glide fly with little effort by floating and rising on air currents

Atlas moth

Atlas moths live in Asia. They are the world's biggest moths. Their wingspan can reach nearly 30 centimetres (1 foot) across. The tips of their wings have a pattern like a snake's head. This may help to scare off predators.

Adult atlas moths only live for about a week. They have just enough time to **mate** and lay eggs.

mate join with another to produce young

Fact! Adult atlas moths do not have fully formed mouths. They do not need to eat during their short adult lives.

Snowy owl

Snowy owls live in Europe, Asia and North America. White and grey feathers help them hide in frozen forests and fields. This predator quietly watches for prey, such as mice.

Snowy owls make nests on the ground. They protect their young fiercely. They even fight animals as large as wolves to protect their young.

Fact! To protect its nest, a snowy owl may pretend to be hurt. This tricks the predator into following the owl away from the nest.

Hammerhead bat

The hammerhead bat has a wingspan of up to 97 centimetres (38 inches). Africa's largest bat swoops through dark skies. When they want to mate, males put on a show. They make honking noises and flap their huge wings. The hammerhead bat mostly eats fruit such as figs.

Glossary

adapt change to fit into a new or different environment

continent one of Earth's seven large land masses

glide fly with little effort by floating and rising on air currents

habitat place where an animal can find its food, water, shelter and space to live

mate join with another to produce young

predator animal that hunts other animals for food

prey animal that is hunted by other animals for food

talon raptor's sharp, curved claw; each toe has a talon

wingspan distance between the tips of a pair of wings when fully open

Find out more

Books

Birds (Fact Cat), Izzi Howell (Wayland, 2016)

Birds of Prey (Kingfisher Readers), Claire Llewellyn (Kingfisher, 2017)

Owls, Laura Marsh (National Geographic, 2014)

Websites

www.dkfindout.com/uk/animals-and-nature/bats/inside-bat
Explore inside the body of a bat!

www.rspb.org.uk/birds-and-wildlife/bird-and-wildlife-guides/bird-a-z/g/goldeneagle/index.aspx
Find out where and when you can see golden eagles in the UK.

Comprehension questions

1. Which animal in this book usually eats small insects and animals, but has been known to attack animals as large as deer?

2. How does an Atlas moth's appearance help protect it from predators?

3. The snowy owl's grey and white feathers make it hard to see in frozen fields. How do you think this helps them when hunting for prey?

Index

CANCELLED